FEET

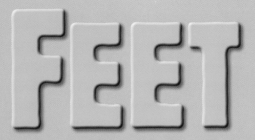

by Melanie Mitchell

first step nonfiction

Lerner Publications · Minneapolis

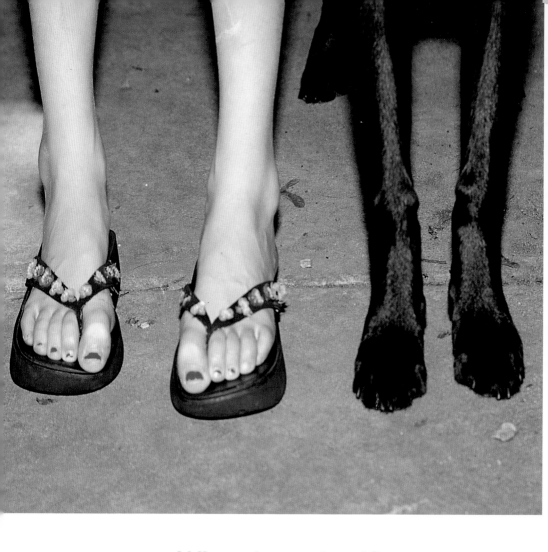

Who has feet?

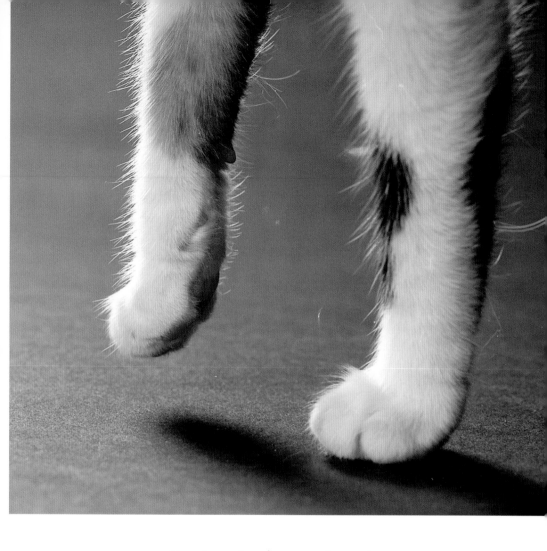

Cats have feet.

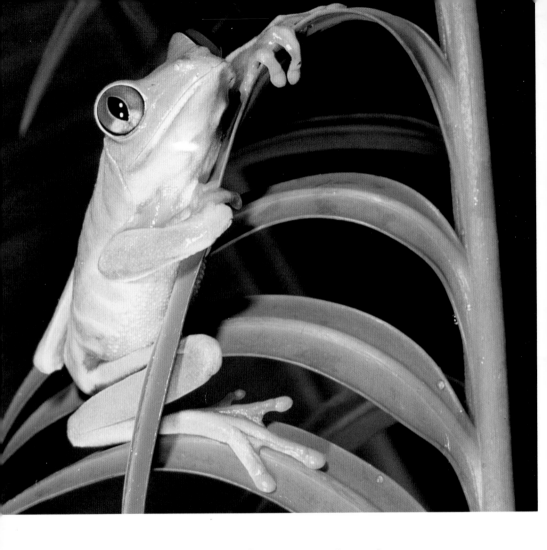

Frogs have feet.

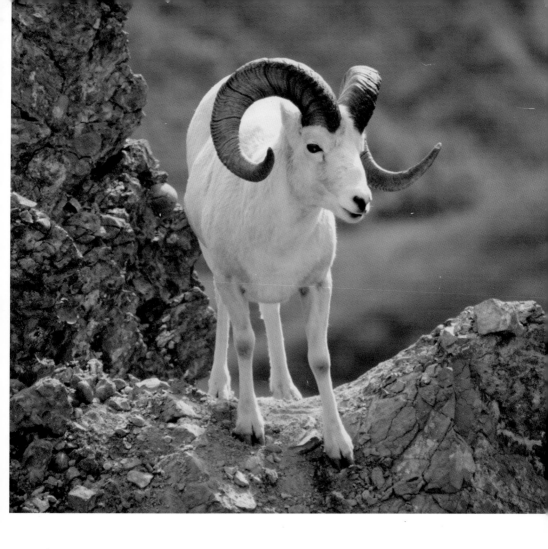

Goats have feet.

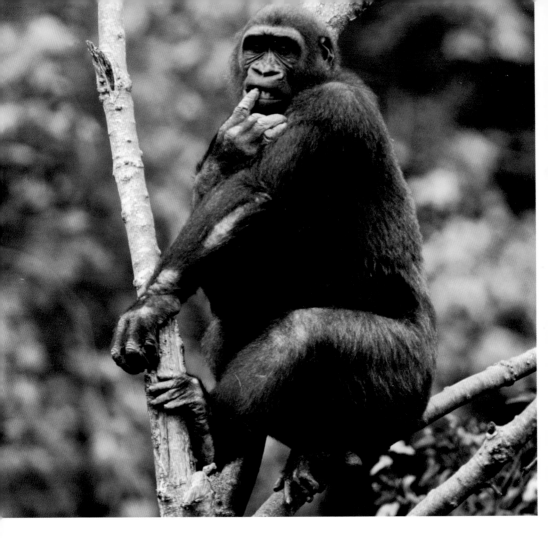

Monkeys have feet.

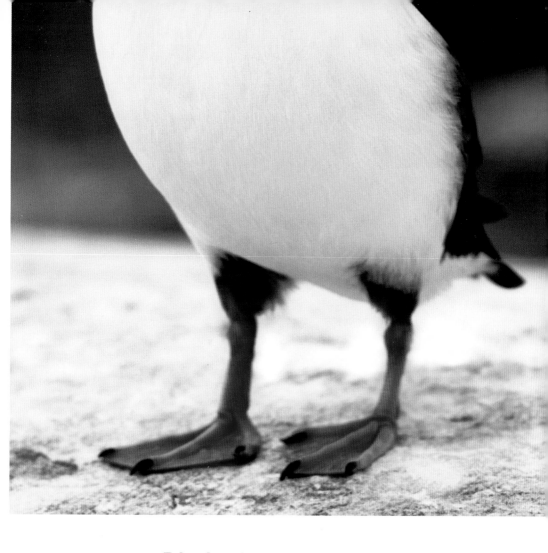

Birds have feet.

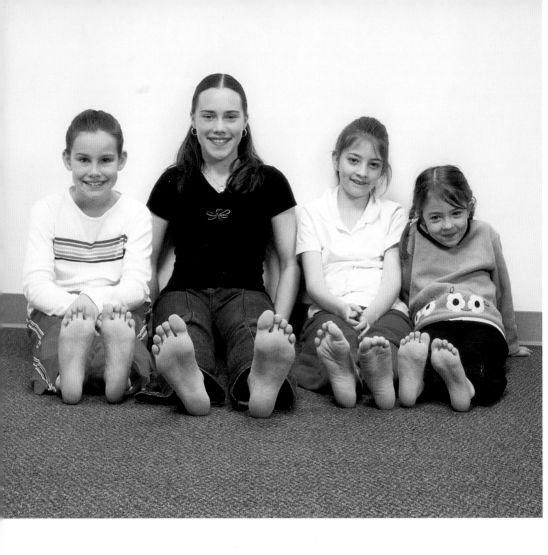

We have feet!